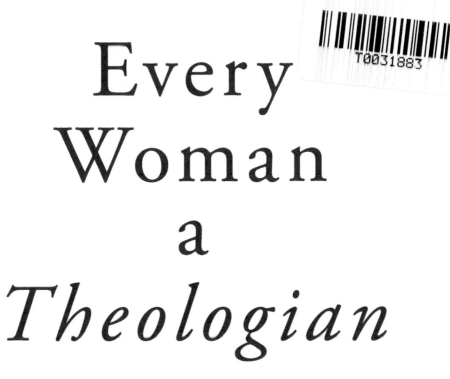

Every Woman a Theologian

KNOW WHAT YOU BELIEVE.
LIVE IT CONFIDENTLY.
COMMUNICATE IT GRACIOUSLY.

WORKBOOK

PHYLICIA MASONHEIMER

HarperChristian
Resources

Every Woman a Theologian Workbook
© 2023 by Phylicia Masonheimer

Requests for information should be addressed to:
HarperChristian Resources, 3900 Sparks Dr. SE, Grand Rapids, Michigan 49546

ISBN 978-0-310-15027-5 (softcover)
ISBN 978-0-310-15028-2 (ebook)

HarperChristian Resources titles may be purchased in bulk for church, business, fundraising, or ministry use. For information, please e-mail ResourceSpecialist@ ChurchSource.com.

The author is represented by Alive Literary Agency, www.aliveliterary.com.

First Printing February 2023 / Printed in the United States of America

CONTENTS

BEFORE WE BEGIN

A Note from Phylicia Masonheimer

Dear Reader,

I'm Phylicia. Maybe this is the first time you and I have crossed paths, or maybe you're here because of my website or podcast. Either way, I am so glad that you are here. I want to get even deeper into His Word with you.

The purpose of this companion workbook is to give me a way to walk with you through this material, helping you take this content from head knowledge to heart change. This workbook is crafted to help you process through and bring to life the practical application of every chapter of the book *Every Woman a Theologian*. It is my greatest hope that you work through this material with a group, be it your neighbors, girlfriends, small group from church, or just your best friend.

There are steps you can follow in the back of this workbook to guide you through using this workbook for a group study. What would be even more incredible, though, is if you work through this material as you read the book and *then* you call together a group of women and you lead them through this workbook! Any way you engage will bear fruit. But, like I said before, we want to move from head knowledge to a heart change. We want these new understandings to take shape in our lives.

Alright. Let's get started! I can't wait to do this with you.

Phylicia
Masonheimer

A Roadmap to the Workbook

So, right now, I'm going to give you a roadmap to the workbook.

In Each Lesson

Heads up! The exercises and questions in each workbook lesson are written with the understanding that you have already read the corresponding chapter in the *Every Woman a Theologian* book.

- **Opening Prayer:** The only way to begin study is with a prayer—short, sincere, and trusting. The Lord is there listening the whole way through.

- **Vocabulary Review:** Maybe you haven't done this since high school, but there is something so important about defining our words: what exactly are we trying to say anyway?

- **Know What You Believe:** A tailored-to-this study how-to section for your Bible study practices. Have you ever used a concordance? Have you ever even wanted to? Well, get ready!

- **Head Knowledge:** I'll ask some questions that explore the terms we just defined and ask for some details of your own experiences.

- **Heart Change:** I provide more questions that build on your head knowledge and cause you to wrestle with your own understanding. These are not about finding the right answer—these are about a willingness to ask God for more insight into your own life and how to change yourself by the Spirit's power to become ever more like Christ. He's ready whenever you are.

- **Theologian's Questions:** In this section, you'll write a few of your own questions, but you won't leave them here. You'll plan on seeking answers by taking them to other believers or doing further research.

- **Common Ground:** Remember how I said this study could be done as a group? These questions were written for the group experience, though they can be used in one-on-one situations or even individually.

- **Live It Boldly:** Answering questions is great, but what are you going to DO about it? This section focuses on orthopraxy, that is, the right practice of Christianity. This section provides a space for you to work out specific, practical ways you want this teaching to influence and change your life. What, exactly, are you going to *do* about these teachings?

- **Moving Forward:** Space is provided for you to track your progress throughout the study, to record prayer requests and praises, and to plan your times of study for the next week.

- **Thanksgiving:** A space to thank God for His word, this study, and your group (if you are a part of one).

LESSON
ONE

INTRODUCTION AND BIBLIOLOGY

The Very Breath of God

KNOW WHAT
YOU BELIEVE.

LIVE IT
CONFIDENTLY.

COMMUNICATE
IT GRACIOUSLY.

LESSON
ONE

INTRODUCTION AND BIBLIOLOGY

Just a reminder: the exercises below are based on the introduction and chapter one: Bibliology in *Every Woman a Theologian* (or *EWAT*).

Opening Prayer

You did it—you're here! Begin your time of study by taking this verse to prayer: ". . . so is my [the Lord's] word that goes out from my mouth: It will not return to me empty, but will accomplish what I desire and achieve the purpose for which I sent it." (Isaiah 55:11)

Write a few lines of prayer thanking God for this truth and asking that His purposes would be accomplished in you.

_____

_____

_____

_____

_____

Vocabulary Review

The basics—they really do matter! Let's start by defining our terms, which are all found in definition boxes in chapter one of the book. The best way to learn these definitions is to write them out one more time.

Theology: _____

Humanism: _____

Bibliology: _____

Canon: _____

Genre: _____

Know What You Believe
How to Use a Bible Commentary

Have you ever read a Bible passage and then thought to yourself, "What in the world was that about?"

Don't worry. You're not the only one. Take your confusion as an encouraging sign of two things: one, you are actually paying attention, and two, you're not letting your own assumptions fill in the holes. But you don't have to live in confusion. Take a moment to consult a Bible dictionary or concordance—or maybe both! These books are typically heavy reference books with teeny, tiny font. Don't let that intimidate you. These books are *for you*. Also, there are amazing dictionary and concordance resources online, so you don't have to worry about the font size anymore!

The purpose of these two types of books is to provide context for the Bible passages that you're reading. They'll give you more information that hopefully will help shed some light on God's word. Bible dictionaries give historical context and Bible concordances give literary context. My favorites are *Strong's Exhaustive Concordance* and *Zondervan Bible Dictionary.*

Any good Bible dictionary will provide you with maps, pictures, and in-depth descriptions. It turns out that knowing something about warfare in ancient times will help you read the biblical books of history with more understanding and appreciation.

A concordance will help you look deeply at the meaning of the particular words in the passage. It will offer cross-references, or other verses that use the same word, to help you understand the meaning of that word in that passage. A concordance is an extremely helpful resource if you're trying to understand the author's original intent with their book, letter, or poem.

Just remember that these dictionaries and concordances are for anyone who wants to understand the Bible with more comprehensive context—these tools are for you. Use them!

Head Knowledge

Let's explore our terms and talk about your own experiences. I'm interested in where you are—both right now and where you've been before.

What's your personal reaction to being called a "theologian"? Does that title fit you? Why or why not?

_____

_____

Where do theologians begin? Look near the end of the chapter.

_____

_____

Take a moment to remember a time you defended your faith. What was the circumstance (speaking to a fellow believer, or non-believer, or someone whom you did not know their perspective)? How did that feel? How were you received? What went well and what perhaps could have been improved upon?

_____

_____

_____

_____

_____

_____

Consider the different genres of the Bible. Which genre appeals to you the most? The least? Which genre do you want to know more about?

Heart Change

It's time to dig deeper. Read through all of these questions before you get started. Start with the one that appeals to you the most. You're wrestling, not answering questions on a test. Start with the question that has a meaningful link into your day-to-day experiences. You'll know it when you see it.

The Bible was not received as a one-time revelation, but in multiple books across both eras and genres. What aspects does Scripture gain because of the way that it was developed?

The Bible is the *kanon* (or measure) that informs everything else about us; for example, political beliefs, identity, and sexuality. Why do you think that this standard is so often "flipped," i.e., identity informing the interpretation of Scripture?

What's the difference between plenary and verbal inspiration?

Theologian's Questions

What unanswered questions do you have about theology? What piqued your curiosity in this chapter? What caused confusion? Write these questions down so you can find out more by asking them to other believers or pursuing them in further research.

Common Ground

These questions are written for group discussion, but they can be used in individual study or as conversation starters. As we travel from head knowledge to heart change, we start reaching out toward others in conversation, searching for common ground.

Everyone, whether they know it or not, is walking around with a theology. What contributes to a person's theological formation—what influences why a person believes what they believe?

_____

_____

_____

How was Scripture received during the time it was written? In other words, who received these words and how did they receive it? How long was it before the words of Scripture were considered inspired?

_____

_____

_____

What is the significance of the discovery of the Dead Sea Scrolls?

_____

_____

_____

_____

Scripture is infallible, that is, unable to deceive, but teachers are not. What kinds of accountability measures do we need to have in place for the people who teach us Scripture? What are some of the signs exhibited by good teachers—how can we recognize who they are?

The Bible says that morality is not subjective. This has always been difficult for the world to accept. We've been trying to determine our own rules since the beginning. Often, conversations about this can be paralyzed by conflicting emotions from both sides. Look again at Phy's conversation in the introduction. How did she lead into her differing opinion? How can we discuss the idea of objective morality with a hostile culture?

For the Christian, what is the purpose of the Bible?

Live It Boldly

So . . . what are you going to DO about it?

The Bible is God's word given to us. It is alive and living. In a very real way, the Bible is God's voice. So, where is your Bible? Not right now. I mean, right now, it's probably on your lap or table or the arm of your chair. Where do you usually keep it? Could you keep it in a place that reminded you to use it more often?

We have the opportunity to hear the voice of God every single day, if only we are willing to open up the Bible. Consider practical and realistic ways you want to incorporate God's voice into your daily life. Write them here, not as mere goals, but promises to yourself to get to know God more deeply and intimately over the course of the next eight weeks.

Moving Forward

What worked well for you this week?

What obstacles did you have to overcome?

Where can you see some walls coming down?

What is one thing of praise you received this week or learned that brought freedom or joy?

Thanksgiving

God, your character is the canon by which all truth is measured. Your Word does not return to you empty. Thank You for the work Your Word is already doing in my life. Help me to look to You as I lift up these requests to you. Remind me to be grateful for the graces and blessings You've poured out on me.

Scan this QR code for a free summary video from Phy!

LESSON
TWO

THEOLOGY

A Loving and Holy Father

KNOW WHAT
YOU BELIEVE.

LIVE IT
CONFIDENTLY.

COMMUNICATE
IT GRACIOUSLY.

LESSON
T W O

THEOLOGY

Opening Prayer

God, you are a loving Father. John writes in 1 John 4:7, "Beloved, let us love one another, for love is from God, and whoever loves has been born of God and knows God" (ESV). I want to be born of You and to know You. By understanding You better, I want to love others more. Help me to accept Your love, to rest in Your love, and to share Your love with others around me. Thank You for this time You've given me to study.

Vocabulary Review

Once again, we're going to start by writing out definitions for our terms. It's going to make sense later, but right now just follow along. Please flip all the way back in the *EWAT* book to the conclusion; there are two terms on the second page of the conclusion that will be important the entire way through the study. The best way to learn these definitions is to write them out in your own words.

Orthodoxy: _____

Orthopraxy: _____

Know What You Believe
How to Use a Bible Commentary

What's your general approach to religious controversy? Some people love digging into the differences between denominations while other people find themselves really uncomfortable when they hit on conflict between Christian beliefs in a real-life context. No matter where you'd place yourself along that spectrum, using a Bible commentary will enliven your experience of Scripture.

I bring up the differences between denominational beliefs because these differences play out strongly in Bible commentaries. These are (often lengthy) books that contain an author's "comments" (hence, "commentary") on passages of Scripture. The content of the explanations will depend on the author's particular area of expertise (like theology or archaeology) and the author's denominational beliefs.

Before you dive into any commentary, ask yourself these questions:

- Where did this author attend seminary/school?

- What other books has this author written?

- Who endorses this author? Who have they endorsed?

As you are reading, ask yourself these questions:

- Does this make me uncomfortable? Why?

- Am I uncomfortable because of my own denominational pre-suppositions, or is there something unbiblical at work here?

Reading through a commentary will likely make you feel uncomfortable. The author may adamantly insist the truth of some theological point that you disagree with. That's uncomfortable—after all, they wrote a commentary, and you probably haven't. I want to encourage you to sit with that discomfort. That discomfort is pointing you toward something, and it's not pointing toward saying to yourself: "you're wrong and stupid." Let me just say it: "you're wrong and stupid" is not something our Father would say to you. That's coming from somewhere else. Instead, discomfort is a sign of growth. It's going to propel you to ask more questions, which is exactly what our good Father would want you to do.

Take your questions and, using the following lists to help your research, see if you can find two differing views by different commentators for one of your questions. You'll find that these conservative, traditional theologians agree on many points, but there are differences within Reformed and Non-Reformed points of view.

REFORMED ● John Calvin ● Martin Luther ● Charles Spurgeon ● John MacArthur ● John Piper ● R. C. Sproul and R. C. Sproul Jr. ● Ray Ortlund ● Warren Wiersbe ● Douglas Moo ● Erwin Lutzer ● Douglas Wilson

NON-REFORMED ● C. S. Lewis ● Matt Pinson ● Gordon Fee ● Leighton Flowers ● John Wesley ● Adam Clarke ● Leroy Forlines

● Robert Picirilli ● Stephen Ashby ● Thomas Oden ● Robert Coleman ● Timothy Tennent

These authors all have incredible insights into Scripture. No matter what your approach to conflict usually is, commentaries will help you grow. After all, reading a commentary is not about "being right." It's about growing in your knowledge of God. It's about appealing to the wisdom He's granted to great thinkers through the ages. It's about who He—our loving, holy Father—really is.

Head Knowledge

Let's explore our terms and talk about our own experiences. I am only where I am today because of the things that I experienced, even though I couldn't understand the pain at the time. I want to hear how Christ has come through for you. Or maybe you feel like He's left you hanging; I want to know about that too.

How has Christ come to you in your loneliness?

_____

_____

Have you ever thought of God as "reluctant?" What have you believed Him reluctant to do in your life?

_____

_____

Have you seen Jesus and God presented as opposites in, for example, media presentations, or in the beliefs of parents and teachers who taught you about God?

_____

_____

When you read the word "community," what kind of feelings arise in you? What does the experience of community look like in your life?

_____

_____

Heart Change

It's time to dig deeper. Read through all of these questions before you get started. Start with the one that appeals to you the most. You're wrestling, not answering questions on a test. Start with the question that has a meaningful link into your day-to-day experiences. You'll know it when you see it.

Michael Reeves wrote this about the Trinity: "And so, because the Christian God is triune, the Trinity is the governing center of all Christian belief".[1] What is your personal theology of the Trinity? How would you explain it to someone who asked you? What questions remain unanswered in your mind about this central Christian doctrine?

_____

_____

_____

----

1 Michael Reeves, _Delighting in the Trinity_ (Downers Grove: InterVarsity Press, 2012).

How do God's definition of love (see 1 John 1:4–7) and our culture's definition of love differ from one another?

_____

_____

_____

Why do some people think of God as self-interested? Can you see the evidence for that argument? Can you see evidence that contradicts that argument?

_____

_____

_____

Theologian's Questions

What unanswered questions do you have about theology? What piqued your curiosity in this chapter? What caused confusion? Write these questions down so you can find out more by asking them to other believers or pursuing them in further research.

_____

_____

_____

_____

_____

Common Ground

These questions are written for group discussion, but they can be used in individual study or as conversation starters. As we travel from head knowledge to heart change, we start reaching out toward others in conversation, searching for common ground. Remember, common ground doesn't mean that all of our circumstances and opinions are the same. In fact, common ground is built on the possibility of talking together, even when we don't agree on all points.

Often it is difficult experiences that drive people toward God. Of course, difficult circumstances may instead have the opposite effect. Why do some people reach for God in difficult times and others start moving away from Him?

What analogies have you heard used to describe the Trinity? What are the strengths and failings of those analogies?

Have you ever read any of the Gospels paying particular attention to what Jesus said about God? What kinds of claims does Jesus make about His Father? How does He speak about God? What kinds of surprising or discomforting things does He say about His Father?

_____

_____

_____

God is just. What injustices do you see in the world around you? What ways do you see Christians disagreeing about the proper administration of justice? God is the loving and holy Father of all Christians—what can we do to come together in our understanding of God's justice?

_____

_____

_____

God's omniscience can truly be a sticky subject. Seriously. Look again at the differences between free-will (Arminianism) and determinism (Calvinism) and start talking about it with each other. Do you notice differences in perspective? How do you present those differences in perspective to each other? Do you notice a difference between asking questions and making statements? Try it!

_____

_____

_____

Why does "open theism" fall short of our loving and Holy Father?

_____

_____

_____

Know What You Believe and Live It Boldly

So . . . what are you going to DO about it?

Let's get into orthodoxy and orthopraxy. I made you flip all the way to the back of the book for some definitions right at the beginning of the study. I want you to read the two paragraphs right below those definition boxes, too.

Orthodoxy is right Christian belief, but orthodoxy without orthopraxy (right Christian living) is going to be . . . well, noisy, for one thing. We could say all the right things, but if we don't back up any of it with right living, do we love God or others at all?

Consider this an invitation to step into maturity. Mature faith doesn't need to be noticed for doing something good. Mature faith doesn't need someone to agree with their point. Mature faith doesn't need to be asked before reaching out.

This week, pray for an opportunity to get some orthopraxy practice. Maybe you could practice grace with someone you disagree with, or plan on doing something good that you will get no thanks for.

Maybe you could seek out a need instead of just responding to them. Write your ideas for orthopraxy below.

_____

_____

_____

_____

Moving Forward

What worked well for you this week?

_____

_____

What obstacles did you have to overcome?

_____

_____

Where can you see some walls coming down?

_____

_____

What is one thing of praise you received this week or learned that brought freedom or joy?

_____

_____

_____

Thanksgiving

God, you are a loving and holy and infinite father. You are all-knowing, all-powerful, and all-good. There is more of You to understand than I will ever be able to understand in a lifetime. Thank You for the infinite possibilities of eternity, and for your promises of love for me. Thank you for being my Father.

Scan this QR code for a free summary video from Phy!

LESSON
THREE

COSMOLOGY

A Beautiful, Broken World

KNOW WHAT
YOU BELIEVE.

LIVE IT
CONFIDENTLY.

COMMUNICATE
IT GRACIOUSLY.

COSMOLOGY

Just a reminder: the exercises below are based on chapter three: Cosmology in *EWAT*.

Opening Prayer

In Your word, God, I read, "In the beginning, God created the heavens and the earth" (Genesis 1:1). I've heard these words so many times, and I long to understand them more fully. I believe that You are my creator and the sustainer of my life. I believe that You created me not just with power but with a clear intention, desiring to express who You are through me. God, Creator of everything, create in my heart a new understanding as I study this week.

Vocabulary Review

You know the drill by now—we start by defining our terms. Hopefully this exercise has brought some clarity to you in the other lessons.

Sometimes, the only thing that we need to take the next step in understanding is a solid definition.

Cosmology: _____

Theism: _____

Anthropology: _____

Hamartiology: _____

Know What You Believe

How to Create a Bible Study Routine

The thing that gets me most excited about the creation story is not any of the details—it's the heart that I've started to see behind those details. In the backdrop of the creation story is God's intentionality. All of the beautiful aspects of the world—the plants, and the animals, and the humans, too—sprang out of God's desire to create it. He did it—all of it—on purpose and because He wanted to. We are truly greatly desired. Do you think of yourself that way? I hope you do. Maybe this week's study will help you see yourself that way.

Not only are we greatly desired, we are designed to be images of God—to be like Him in our aspects. As God created the world out of nothing, He also gave us the desire to bring order out of chaos on the smaller frame of our lives.

Now's when I'm going to talk about your own Bible study routine.

Maybe "order out of chaos" rings particularly true for you on this subject, or maybe you already have a strong study routine. Either way, I want to offer some advice for creating on a scale that is smaller than the cosmos.

The first thing you need to do is repeat after me:

I can study the Bible in imperfect circumstances.

I'm going to say it again. Feel free to yell it if you need to:

I CAN STUDY THE BIBLE IN IMPERFECT CIRCUMSTANCES.

No matter how great your plan is on paper, if you are threatened by the imperfections and interruptions of daily life, you will never, ever be able to stick to a Bible study routine. It doesn't matter what phase of life you're in, there will always be other demands on your time. You will always have to *choose* to study. So, when plans change, or the phone suddenly rings, or the baby starts to cry, remember (and say it with me again!): I can study the Bible in imperfect circumstances.

Alright. Now that we've got that down, here are my best tips on creating a great Bible study routine:

- **Make it the first thing you do** (or close to the first thing you do). I usually work out before I sit down to study the Bible, but I still prioritize study for the first part of the morning. If I study before I do (almost) anything else, I will be more likely to do it every day.

- **Stick with the same location.** It should be comfortable but not too comfortable—especially in the early morning, you need a location that helps you stay alert.

- **Keep your materials together.** The last thing you need is to spend precious time scrambling for a highlighter at 6 a.m. Keep a few writing utensils (I love highlighters) and a Bible and journal (and, for now, *EWAT* and this workbook!) in a basket. Keep the basket in the same place. It'll be ready for you every day.

- **You already have routines—piggyback!** Do you drink coffee every morning? Maybe you're more of a tea person. Try to identify something that you already do every morning—could you incorporate your time of study into something you're already doing every day? I mean, reading even one verse out of the Bible beats scrolling through the feed on your phone.

Remember, God creates and keeps creating in circumstances that were rendered imperfect. It's not going to be easy to start or maintain a routine like this, but you've been imprinted with the desire and the ability to create order out of your own morning chaos. You can do it. (And if you're already doing it, you can keep doing it!)

Head Knowledge

Let's think some more expansive thoughts related to our terms and take a moment to harken back to our own personal experiences. As children, we were accomplished cosmologists. It's time to get back in that headspace—at least for a little while—and wonder. It's time to think back to the first time that we heard the story of how the world was made.

What do you remember about the creation stories you were told as a child?

There seems to be a link between cosmology and childlikeness. What attributes do children have that make them more willing to think about the beginning of time and the purpose of the universe?

This chapter presents the opposite of creation as "accusation." Satan is the "adversary" or the accuser, the one who works against creation. In your own life, how has accusation been destructive?

Especially when considering original sin, have you ever thought of God as unreasonable?

Heart Change

Heart change means digging deep. Read through all of these questions before you get started. Start with the one that appeals to you the most. You're wrestling, not answering questions on a test. Start with the question that has a meaningful link into your day-to-day experiences. You'll know it when you see it.

Father Irenaeus, one of the church fathers, describes the process of creation, saying, "And as God is verbal, therefore, He made created things by the Word [Jesus]; and God is Spirit, so that He adorned all things by the Spirit." Find the whole quote in *EWAT* (p 49) and pray with it, allowing yourself to be awed by the mystery of the Trinity. What are the differences between establishing, creating, and adorning? How do you see each of the persons of the Trinity as involved in the act of creation?

From the standpoint of cosmology, why is idolatry so offensive to God?

It is easy to wonder how God thought of sin in the first place. Couldn't something else have been done? Phy writes regarding God and sin, "Although He foresaw it, He did not cause it. He did not plan it. He risked it" (page 57 in the book). What is the difference between "planning it" and "risking it"? What does someone who says God planned sin believe about God's heart? What does someone who says God risked sin believe about God's heart?

Theologian's Questions

What unanswered questions do you have about theology? What piqued your curiosity in this chapter? What caused confusion? Write these questions down so you can find out more by asking them to other believers or pursuing them in further research.

_____

_____

_____

_____

_____

Common Ground

These questions are written for group discussion, but they can be used in individual study or as conversation starters. These questions— where did we come from and why were we created?—are appealing to a wide range of individuals, and to a wide range of beliefs that all fall under the umbrella of "Christian." Ask the Holy Spirit for guidance. Assert the truth, of course, but do so in love. And always remember to listen.

What is the link between cosmology and objective morality?

_____

_____

_____

Creation theories abound among Christians living today, just as theories abounded among our Christian ancestors. Do you know of any other creation theories in addition to the ones listed in this chapter? What is the core of cosmology, and what does that core teach us about the heart of God?

_____

_____

_____

Where does our value as human beings come from, and is it possible to destroy that value?

_____

_____

_____

In James 4:17, we read, "If anyone, then, knows the good they ought to do and doesn't do it, it is sin for them." Humans experience a sense of conscience about whether an action is right or wrong. Where does this sense of "ought to do" come from, and what does it say about humans? What does it say about God?

_____

_____

_____

Theologian John Wesley said, "The power to resist grace is of grace." What large-scale resistances to grace do you see in the world? What small-scale resistances to grace do humans enact in their own lives? Juxtapose those resistances to Wesley's quote. Where is God in the human ability to not receive His grace?

_____

_____

_____

Our Adamic ancestors made a choice to align with hopelessness. What practical avenues do we have to align with hope? Have you ever experienced disillusionment when you thought you were doing something creative and hopeful? What did you do about that disillusionment?

_____

_____

_____

Live It Boldly

So . . . what are you going to DO about it?

Let's get into orthodoxy and orthopraxy again. This is one of my favorite things to talk about, because great theology in practice with true Christian behavior points people directly toward Christ. For now, flip back to the conclusion in the book and read the paragraphs under the heading, "The Rise of the Ungracious Christian."

Have you experienced tense conversations around the topic of creation? I've seen a fair number of barbs and responses that I would place firmly in the category of the "ungracious Christian." The zeal for expressing theology to others can get twisted by pride. Think about this quote from Francis Shaeffer: "Biblical orthodoxy without compassion is surely the ugliest thing in the world."

This week, pray for an opportunity to get some orthopraxy practice. Pray for the chance to be a gracious Christian. Write a prayer for the chance to share biblical orthodoxy—right teaching—with compassion, as true an expression of orthopraxy as there is!

Moving Forward

What worked well for you this week?

What obstacles did you have to overcome?

Where can you see some walls coming down?

What is one thing of praise you received this week or learned that brought freedom or joy?

_____

_____

Thanksgiving

God, in Your act of creation, You risked everything for my freedom. To You, the possibility of sin was a worthwhile risk, because You wanted me to be like you—free and full of the capacities to love and to create. The beginning—that beginning—was not just the start of the world, it was the start of the possibility of my relationship with You. Thank You for creating the world with that possibility in Your heart.

Scan this QR code for a free summary video from Phy!

LESSON
FOUR

CHRISTOLOGY

And He Dwelt among Us

KNOW WHAT
YOU BELIEVE.

LIVE IT
CONFIDENTLY.

COMMUNICATE
IT GRACIOUSLY.

LESSON
FOUR

CHRISTOLOGY

Just a reminder: the exercises below are based on chapter four: Christology in *EWAT*.

Opening Prayer

Jesus, in front of a hostile crowd, you stated boldly "If I glorify myself, my glory means nothing. My Father, whom you claim as your God, is the one who glorifies me'" (John 8:54). To claim God as my God, I must claim you as God, too. During this time of study, I want to wonder anew about Your humanity and divinity. I want to know more of who You are—You before time, You in Your humanity, and You glorified.

Vocabulary Review

Let's begin by defining our terms. For many of us, Christology is the study of looking at the Jesus we have known since childhood and reconsidering what those familiar words—humanity, deity, incarnation—really mean. The base of this new understanding is writing out definitions of our terms again.

Christology: _____

Incarnation: _____

Know What You Believe

How to Choose and Use a Reading Plan

This chapter on Christology makes one thing very, very clear: to know the story of the Bible, and the God who speaks it as His word, we have to know the whole thing. Old Testament, New Testament, prophecies, psalms, gospels, and epistles—they all testify to one triune God. The Gospels purposefully point back to the prophecies. The writers of the epistles were well versed in the Law. Pieces of the Psalms point toward major moments of the Gospels.

It's not just sixty-six random books that you once memorized the titles of—it's all connected and it all points toward Christ.

So, have you read it?

This is a great time for an honest answer. This isn't about passing a test; this is about you growing closer to God's heart. Reading the entire Bible is a great way to grow closer to God and to let go of any misconceptions about the identity of Jesus.

If you've read it, let me encourage you: do it again. I've done it several times, and each time, there has been something new and beautiful and fruitful.

If you've never done it, I've got great news for you: you can do it.

But don't try to do it on your own. Using a reading plan is the best way to make it through the entire Bible. Starting at Genesis and pushing all the way through to Revelation, however many chapters you can stomach at a time, is not very sustainable.

Using a reading plan isn't "cheating"—it's just like using a recipe in the kitchen. Someone else already thought of the ingredients and the steps. You don't have to make those decisions, you can just focus on cooking. It's the same thing here. Take an inventory of all the amazing apps and websites that are available to you and find a plan that is going to be supportive of your journey through the entire Bible. There are even Bible-in-a-year podcasts, where the host reads part of the Bible in listenable chunks.

But while we're on the topic of in-a-year, let me give you one key to success when it comes to using your Bible reading plan: let the time frame go. This isn't a race. It isn't a contest. This is about you encountering Scripture—all of it—for yourself. And, truth be told, if you're not so desperate to "do it in a year," you might be more likely to do it. The pressure's off, but the purpose is on.

If reading through the Bible—according to any plan—has never worked for you before, here's what I'd recommend:

- Read or listen to the Bible every day, and do deeper study and notetaking at least three days a week.

- Read through the entire Bible in two years, splitting the year-long plan's selected readings in half each day.

- Read through each book of the Bible in order but take as long as you choose on each book.

And if you get bogged down, or stuck, or if you miss a day, remember: this is not about a streak. It's about growing closer to God. If it's about the streak, you'll get discouraged and discontinue the plan after a few days of missing your reading time. If it's about growing closer to the one who spoke it, you'll be able to return to the reading, even after you miss a day or two.

Head Knowledge

Can you imagine not knowing who Jesus was and what He did? Maybe this is your story, and you came to know Him later in your life. Or maybe you've been hearing about Jesus for as long as you can remember. It's possible to hear something so many times that it's like we've never heard it at all. In this chapter, I want you to hear these truths about Christ—a Jewish carpenter whose name Jesus translates as "Joshua"—with new understanding.

When did you first hear that Christ was God? Have you questioned this in your life?

_____

_____

What kinds of misunderstandings have you heard about Christ? Have you ever experienced a difference of opinion about Christ's identity and importance? What was that like?

_____

_____

This chapter presents six different facets of Christ's identity: Old Testament prophecies, His pre-existence, His humanity, His deity,

His death, and His resurrection. Which of these do you feel you know the most about? The least?

_____

_____

Think of someone you know whom you believe follows Christ. What do they do that makes you believe they follow Him? What reasons do you think they would offer for their belief in Him?

_____

_____

Heart Change

Heart change means digging deep. This time, we're digging into the question of Christ's identity. Who is Christ? Read through these questions before you get started. Start with the one that appeals to you the most. You're wrestling, not answering questions on a test. Start with the question that has a meaningful link into your day-to-day experiences. You'll know it when you see it.

God worked through the history and context of the nation of Israel, a tiny square on today's map. What was His relationship with Israel like? What aspects of God's character does His relationship with Israel reveal to us?

_____

_____

_____

Take a moment to think about Jesus's preexistence: Jesus existed before the creation of the world. Why is this area of Christology so important? If Jesus did not exist before the creation of the world, what would be different about His identity?

Many heresies throughout the centuries have insisted that Jesus was not fully human. Why do you think people have been resistant to the idea of Jesus being human and having human experiences? Do you see any tendencies to "play down" either Jesus's humanity or His divinity in today's culture?

Theologian's Questions

What unanswered questions do you have about theology? What piqued your curiosity in this chapter? What caused confusion? Write these questions down so you can find out more by asking them to other believers or pursuing them in further research.

Common Ground

These questions are written for group discussion, but they can be used in individual study or as conversation starters. If you're ready for an interesting conversation, start talking to other people about who they believe Christ is. Ask the Holy Spirit for guidance, and always remember to listen.

What associations does the word "prophecy" bring to your mind? What do you think of biblical prophecies? In what parts of the Bible would you expect prophecies to be found?

How does an understanding of the Old Testament help us when we're reading the Gospels, particularly when we're trying to understand what Jesus actually says about Himself? Have you ever found that your own cultural assumptions got in the way when you were trying to read Scripture?

Read John 8:54–59 again, assigning at least two people to do the reading, one as Christ, and the other as the crowd. What kinds of expression and action happen when the passage is read aloud?

As apologist J. Warner Wallace wrote, "So while you may not find the expression 'I am God' in the Gospels, you'll certainly find the ancient equivalent." When we read the Bible looking for specific phrases, we often end up disappointed, because we need to understand the larger context to understand the individual verses. Have you looked for a "lacking phrase" in the Bible? Do you think that cultural context would have helped you understand?

Have you ever heard the crucifixion referred to as "cruel" or thought of it that way yourself? What pieces of encouragement does this chapter offer regarding the death of Jesus? According to Scripture, what perspective did Jesus have about His own death—was He willing or unwilling?

The church understands Scripture to teach that Christ's death was sacrificial, substitutionary, redemptive, and victorious. Consider the two different views that this chapter offers about the substitutionary nature of Christ's death. What is the difference between taking a payment and overcoming the powers of evil?

_____

_____

_____

Live It Boldly

So . . . what are you going to DO about it?

Orthopraxy, as we've talked about before, is the right practice of Christianity. It's the practice of living our beliefs boldly in our churches and in the world.

So, what do we do when Christ-followers believe different things?

Well, it depends on *what* different things.

First, I want to say this: theological differences are tremendous opportunities to learn from each other. Especially in our culture, which has amped-up the act of disagreement into total internet free-for-all, we tend to think that differences among groups are huge problems instead of interesting opportunities. This includes differences among believers. What do we do with differences? We use theological triage. This is an extremely useful tool given to us by Dr. Albert Mohler, and we'll talk about it in the orthopraxy section of next week, too. For now, flip back to the conclusion in the book, and find "Steps of Theological Triage."

Christology is the perfect chapter for understanding what Dr. Mohler calls "First Order Issues." In addition to the physical life, death, and resurrection of Christ, Dr. Mohler lists the nature of the Trinity, the hope of eternity, the final judgment of sin, the sanctity of worship, the sanctity of life, and the sanctity of sex as "First Order Issues." To step outside of what Scripture teaches about these things constitutes heresy—as it relates to this chapter, to assert that Jesus wasn't fully God (or fully human) would be to step outside of Christianity itself.

This week, pray for an opportunity to get some orthopraxy practice. Write a prayer for the chance to hear from someone who has a different theological perspective and take a moment to consider if that perspective is a "First Order" difference, or not.

Moving Forward

What worked well for you this week?

What obstacles did you have to overcome?

Where can you see some walls coming down?

What is one thing of praise you received this week or learned that brought freedom or joy?

Thanksgiving

Jesus, You are God. You are the one who was foretold from the beginning, the One who existed before the beginning. Jeremiah and Isaiah wrote about You, and King David sang about You. Everything points toward Your love for us. You chose to come to earth, fully God and fully man, to die for my sins willingly. And, on the third day You rose again. Thank You for this reality—the reality of the cross—that brings light to everything else.

Scan this QR code for a free summary video from Phy!

LESSON
FIVE

SOTERIOLOGY

No Longer a Slave

KNOW WHAT
YOU BELIEVE.

LIVE IT
CONFIDENTLY.

COMMUNICATE
IT GRACIOUSLY.

SOTERIOLOGY

Just a reminder: the exercises below are based on chapter five: Soteriology in *EWAT*.

Opening Prayer

Jesus, in Paul's letter to Titus, I read, "But when the kindness and love of God our Savior appeared, he saved us, not because of righteous things we had done, but because of his mercy" (Titus 3:4–5a)—Your mercy, not my righteousness. I get wrapped up in doing things "the right way." I often forget that Your mercy *is* my righteousness, and that, to have a deeper understanding of my own salvation, I must trust You and Your mercy. May I trust You more and more.

Vocabulary Review

Let's begin by defining our terms, an especially important discipline as we approach soteriology. As we consider different views on salvation, let's remember that understanding one another well starts with understanding the terms we're using. Find these terms in the chapter and write out the definitions.

Soteriology: _____

Sanctification: _____

Glorification: _____

Know What You Believe

How to Get the Most Out of Your Bible Study

In this chapter, we discussed several different denominations (Roman Catholic, Orthodox, Calvinist, and Arminian) and their views on salvation. Each of these views as expressed by the writers, thinkers, and church fathers from each of these denominations relies on an understanding of Scripture. Reading their work is so important. I'll always stand behind that! In addition to tremendous historical resources, we have access to a wealth of contemporary resources that lead us through the Bible according to the thoughts of specific Bible study teachers. These are amazing ways to grow in knowledge.

However, it is so important to prioritize reading the Bible for ourselves. We are promised that the Holy Spirit (God Himself!) will speak to us when we take in the words of the Bible. Bible study brings us closer to God and increases our own understanding of the gift of salvation. The Bible tells us definitively who He is and what He has done for us.

Maybe you've never before studied the Bible on your own, guide-free. Maybe you're anxious to open it up on your own—after all, what if you don't understand something? What if you do it wrong? Well, remember how the Holy Spirit comes to us in God's Word? Before you start, remember that God is with you. A very simple recognition of God's presence in a prayer before you start reading is the way to put Him first. You showed up, but you're here because He is here. And He wants you to know Him more.

For anyone who's trying to study the Bible for the first time, here are the three ways I recommend that you approach God's Word:

Be Intentional!

Intentional Bible students don't expect the Bible to speak to them by randomly flipping to a page. They choose a place to start. They learn how to break down passages, where to look when they have questions, and to set a time for digging deep. Intentionality tip: don't risk forgetting where you were! **Bookmark** that passage.

Be Thoughtful!

Thoughtful Bible students are always asking questions of the text: "Who is this talking to or about? Where else in the Bible is this mentioned? Why did the author say this?" Thoughtfulness tip: use **highlighters and pens** to interact with the text. Don't worry about "messing it up."

Be Disciplined!

Disciplined Bible students don't wait to feel like studying before they make the Word of God a priority. They know that emotions come and go; they change and shift, but we are changed by coming to the Word regardless of our feelings. Let feelings follow actions rather than drive them! Discipline tip: set that alarm clock **15 minutes early**. You can make time with God a priority.

Ask the Holy Spirit to help you be intentional, thoughtful, and disciplined as you study God's Word. In our practice of study, just like with our understanding of salvation, we can get wrapped up in what "doing it right" looks like. Reading the Bible is an act of trust—trust that these words truly are God's words. We don't need to "do it right" out of fear. We can open up the Bible with great hope, knowing that God wants us to trust Him.

Head Knowledge

Salvation is the central theme of Christian testimonies, or stories of how people came to faith in Christ. Testimonies are shared around the dinner table, around the campfire, and in intimate conversation. This chapter included the description of our Christian heritage as a huge, spreading family tree. That tree is full of stories of salvation, of interactions with soteriology. These stories are all beautifully different and wondrously alike. Let's consider your own story of salvation. I came to Christ (or, rather, He came to me) at age 16. What about you?

If someone asked you how you were saved, what would you say? Has your answer changed over time? If so, how?

What are the three aspects of salvation that Phy writes about?

Has your freedom in Christ changed the way that you live? How has it changed you? How have you seen that freedom change others around you?

_____

_____

Reflect for a minute on *manumissio vindicta*, the Roman ceremony that is explained in the beginning of the chapter. Place Jesus in the role of the owner, and yourself in the role of the slave.

_____

_____

Heart Change

Heart change means digging deep. Soteriology offers plentiful opportunities to dig deeper into concepts. You've heard about being saved, but how exactly does that work? Welcome the mystery. Make room for the questions. And don't feel bad if you feel like you don't understand something. That means that God is getting you ready for some serious growth. Read through these questions before you get started. Start with the question that has a meaningful link into your day-to-day experiences. You'll know it when you see it.

Let's work through the four theological perspectives on salvation. Instead of just re-writing what is already in the chapter, choose a key word and relate what you learned about each denomination to that key word. Here are three sample key words you could choose. You can also come up with your own key word.

RESPONSE   GRACE   ATONEMENT

Roman Catholic

_____

_____

Eastern Christianity

_____

_____

Calvinistic Reformed

_____

_____

Arminian-Wesleyan and Anabaptist

_____

_____

To the secular world, Christianity is often associated with keeping up appearances, playing by the rules, and generally disliking people who are not part of the "club." What aspects of Christianity and soteriology are twisted into this wrong understanding?

_____

_____

_____

There are two other "stages" of salvation, other than that first stage of coming to faith. Describe these two stages. What can be done here and now? What are we still waiting for? What kinds of habits and actions grow from understanding the "mid-game" and "end-game" of salvation?

_____

_____

_____

Theologian's Questions

What unanswered questions do you have about theology? What piqued your curiosity in this chapter? What caused confusion? Write these questions down so you can find out more by asking them to other believers or pursuing them in further research.

_____

_____

_____

_____

_____

Common Ground

These questions are written for group discussion, but they can be used in individual study or as conversation starters. If you're ready for an interesting conversation, start talking to other people about who they believe Christ is. Ask the Holy Spirit for guidance, and always remember to listen.

What can we do to promote peace and understanding between denominations? What happens when we confuse "understanding" with "agreement," especially in relationships between churches?

Think of God's judgment from different perspectives: church, cultural, and personal. What images do you see? God raining down fire and brimstone? God, the Judge, seated at the front of a courtroom? A father embracing his son? Where have you seen these perspectives, and what other kinds of perspectives have you seen?

Imagine two different women who needed forgiveness for a terrible mistake. Forgiveness was granted to each woman, but one woman remains preoccupied with her mistake while the other lets go of hers. How will each woman act? What kinds of things will the preoccupied woman do? What kinds of things will the woman who let go do? How will each woman view the person who forgave them?

Why do Christians reject certain behaviors? What does it look like when people or groups of people reject certain behaviors because they are afraid of punishment? How is it different when people are choosing to live in a certain way because they are free?

_____

_____

_____

Consider the phrase, "Identity precedes action." How does this phrase play out in your understanding of salvation?

_____

_____

_____

The Christian life isn't easy. We've all seen the headlines about once-famous-now-notorious pastors and leaders come crashing down into disgrace. We've also seen rifts and burnout and just plain boredom overtake people in our own churches and communities. There is plenty of anecdotal evidence to support the idea that Christianity is not sustainable. What makes the Christian life sustainable? How have you seen Christianity sustained?

_____

_____

_____

_____

Live It Boldly

So . . . what are you going to DO about it?

Orthopraxy, as we've talked about before, is the right practice of Christianity. It's the practice of living our beliefs boldly in our churches and in the world.

So, what do we do when Christ-followers believe different things?

Let's go back to the analogy of the family tree. We talked last week about first-order issues. Think these kinds of questions: Is God triune? Is Jesus fully God and fully man? Is the human person eternal? These kinds of beliefs are the trunk of our family tree. To be a Christian is to believe these things. If you need a good summary of these beliefs, check out the Apostles' Creed.

In this chapter, we dug into denominational differences about soteriology. If you look in the back again at the orthopraxy section, you'll see that Dr. Mohler placed soteriology in the "second order." A difference in second order issues make it difficult to worship under the same roof, but these differences don't divide us into Christian and non-Christian. We may have different opinions and practices regarding baptism, but we agree that it's a vital part of the Christian life. We agree that the Holy Spirit is one of the persons of our triune God, but we understand and express the gifts of the Spirit differently.

We worked through several perspectives on soteriology during this study. Take a little time to familiarize yourself with the second-order issues in the orthopraxy section. Where do you stand on some of these other issues, like communion and women in leadership? And, as a bonus, look up a few perspectives that differ from yours, practicing the idea that understanding is not the same thing as agreement.

_____

_____

_____

_____

Moving Forward

What worked well for you this week?

_____

_____

What obstacles did you have to overcome?

_____

_____

Where can you see some walls coming down?

_____

_____

What is one thing of praise you received this week or learned that brought freedom or joy?

_____

_____

Thanksgiving

Jesus, I claim this truth from Paul's letter to the Galatians: "It is for freedom that Christ has set us free" (Galatians 5:1). You are a compassionate master, not a disinterested judge. You do not merely check my sins off a list and dismiss me; You call me into a greater freedom than I have ever imagined. You say, "I want this woman to be free!" You have offered me the incredible (and completely free!) gift of salvation. Help me to live in the freedom that You have won for me and to know that You long to see me free.

Scan this QR code for a free summary video from Phy!

LESSON
SIX

PNEUMATOLOGY

Like Flames and Doves

KNOW WHAT
YOU BELIEVE.

LIVE IT
CONFIDENTLY.

COMMUNICATE
IT GRACIOUSLY.

PNEUMATOLOGY

Just a reminder: the exercises below are based on chapter six: Pneumatology in *EWAT*.

Opening Prayer

Jesus, you told Your followers, "wait for the gift my Father promised" (Acts 1:4). You had already risen from the dead, but you had even more in store for us. Lord, I'm here, with my hands and my heart open. The gift and the Father are one: the Holy Spirit is God as You are God and the Father is God. I pray that I would understand the Holy Spirit a little more through this week of study.

Vocabulary Review

This week, it's an exercise in defining something that can feel undefinable—the Holy Spirit. As we approach this mystery, let's remember to be grateful for the infinite nature of God. We wouldn't want to worship a God whom we could understand fully. If we recognize and embrace this, all the mystery, all the not-yet-known is truly our security. Let's start by defining pneumatology (from page 111 in the *EWAT* book):

Pneumatology: _____

Know What You Believe

How to Get Started with Inductive Bible Study

One of the most incredible things about the Holy Spirit is how often the Bible talks directly about him. Ideas about the Holy Spirit can be difficult to grasp, but we have been given so much Scripture to work with. The best part is this: it's the Holy Spirit that is going to help us understand what the Bible says about the Holy Spirit. Make sense?

Growing deeper in our knowledge of God and of Scripture requires an in-depth look at God's Word. Inductive Bible study is not just about reading the Bible; it's about working with it and through it. It's about getting active in our approach to studying it. We won't retain anything if we just read it. Don't believe me? Try repeating a passage verbatim out of a book you just read. Maybe you loved the book, but you probably didn't retain anything in exact words.

One of our main goals with reading the Bible is to bring it into our everyday life—our imperfect, sometimes impossible, often messy life. Inductive Bible study conditions your mind to remember the Word in your everyday circumstances. In your next chaotic moment, the thing that pops into your head will be something that you've spent some time focusing on—anxiety, anger, or, maybe, some Scripture.

Wouldn't that last option be wonderful? It is possible. And remember: you have a Helper. Ask for the Holy Spirit's help!

Here are the steps for some inductive study:

Read: The first thing you need to do is read the passage. It's great to read what comes before and what comes after the passage you're working on to get a little context.

Highlight Key Words and Phrases: If you use certain colors to indicate the names of God and Jesus and others to show where words and phrases are repeated. Working with the Bible like this can transform the way that you see the words, and it will help you remember them.

Write Notes: You'll need an extra notebook. The margins of your Bible aren't quite large enough to write down everything that you're going to notice and wonder.

If you're not sure where to start with notetaking, start with these categories:

The 5 Ws and an H:

Who: Key figures, genealogies, family lineage

What: Events, actions, things occurring in the passage

Where: Locations, connections to other locations in Scripture

When: Time of writing and time of occurrence

Why: Motivations of characters, reasoning, past promises

How: How the story played out; what actions were taken?

Ask, "**What do I learn about God in this passage?**" We're looking for the heart of the Father, and the Bible is all about our God. We can get fixated on learning something about ourselves, but the truth is that who He is, is much more important than who we are.

Pray: I always advise asking God to show you how you can live in light of what you've just read. The Word is light in our life, and it is living and active. If you're open to the movements of the Holy Spirit, that light will change everything.

Head Knowledge

What does your daily experience with the Holy Spirit look like? The Holy Spirit is our help, our tireless advocate, and one of the persons of our triune God. It's easy to misunderstand or even forget about the role of the Holy Spirit in our own growth in Christ. Exploring the terms and concepts of this chapter can help you understand the Holy Spirit better and become even more open to grace.

Generally speaking, is it easy or difficult for you to accept help? Does your answer depend on the circumstance? If so, how?

What is the trifold mission of the Holy Spirit in the world?

What's the difference between *continuationist* and *cessationist* churches? Does the church that you attend now fit clearly into one of these categories?

_____

_____

_____

Can you relate to what Phy describes about wanting "checklist Christianity"?

_____

_____

Heart Change

Pneumatology is a very personal topic, full of opportunities for heart change. The Holy Spirit's work in each of us is so personal, but it goes so much further than personality. The grace of the Holy Spirit is for all Christians, though, so let's dig in deep! Read through these questions before you get started. Start with the question that has a meaningful link into your day-to-day experiences. You'll know it when you see it.

Paul writes two different lists of the gifts of the Holy Spirit, one in Romans 12:4–8 and 1 Corinthians 12: 4–11. A combination of these lists is on page 121 of the EWAT book. Paul includes these lists toward the end of his letters to each of these churches. What does the position of these lists tell us about the gifts of the Holy Spirit? How can we differentiate these gifts and recognize them in other people and ourselves without reducing the gifts of the Holy Spirit to some kind of personality test?

What is the purpose of the gifts of the Holy Spirit? How does that purpose play out on individual, relational, and communal levels?

What can a Christian expect if she is following the voice of the Holy Spirit? What kinds of experiences and emotions may not be a part of her experience of obedience?

Theologian's Questions

What unanswered questions do you have about theology? What piqued your curiosity in this chapter? What caused confusion? Write these questions down so you can find out more by asking them to other believers or pursuing them in further research.

_____

_____

_____

_____

Common Ground

These questions are written for group discussion, but they can be used in individual study or as conversation starters. In other workbook lessons, we've asked the Holy Spirit to guide our conversations—we can keep asking for that, even as we're talking about the Holy Spirit!

Do you think of yourself as a rule-follower or an adventurer, or of something in-between? How does this influence your experience of the Holy Spirit's leading?

_____

_____

Choose three or four of the spiritual gifts to focus on. What do each of these gifts teach you about the heart of Christ and the way that he wants us to serve the world?

How have you understood the particular gifts of the Holy Spirit over the course of your life—gifts given to you, to your spouse, to your children? Have you been given different gifts at different times? Has a stage of development (adulthood, parenthood) brought on change in respect to these gifts?

What kinds of danger arise when believers start saying that the Holy Spirit only acts in certain ways? What kinds of opportunities for growth would be missed by someone who thinks the Spirit is only sensational? What kinds of opportunities for growth would be missed by someone who is intimidated by anything that would disrupt the current order?

What things do believers do that grieve the Holy Spirit or frustrate the Holy Spirit's work in their lives or the lives of others around them?

_____

_____

_____

Phy describes prayer as "an ongoing heartfelt conversation." What other four-word definitions of "prayer" can you come up with that specifically call out the communal nature of prayer?

_____

_____

_____

Live It Boldly

So . . . what are you going to DO about it?

Orthopraxy, as we've talked about before, is the right practice of Christianity. It's the practice of living our beliefs boldly in our churches and in the world.

So, what do we do when Christ-followers believe different things?

This is a dynamic we all encounter. We don't have to go much further than Twitter to find Christians disagreeing with one another, but often it's much more personal. We disagree with our real-life neighbors and relatives, too. But to show Christ to the world, we need to live in peace with one another. Note that living in peace with one another does NOT require 100% agreement on all things. It's really the opposite. If we can extend our hands in fellowship to one another without being opinion clones, that really does image Christ's peace to the world. To understand how to disagree with charity and graciousness, we're working through Dr. Mohler's theological triage on page 172 of the book.

First-order issues (like the nature of the Trinity) constitute the basics of Christianity. Second-order issues (like how to practice baptism) divide us into different denominations, but don't separate us into different religions. Third-order issues are differences that often exist within church communities.

You've probably run into the most real-life disagreements about third-order issues like: the end times, modesty, perspectives on parenting, convictions about alcohol, and preferences about media.

The most important thing to remember is this: we can't elevate third-order issues to first-order importance. The inverse is also extremely problematic. Check out Dr. Mohler's incredible quote on page 174 of the book. Consider the ways that some groups err on each of these sides. Consider the ways that you may have downplayed first-order issues or elevated third-order issues. This will take a lot of humility, but it's so good to let the Spirit do this work in us.

Write a prayer for the intervention of the Holy Spirit in your own heart and for an opportunity for some orthopraxy practice this week.

Moving Forward

What worked well for you this week?

_____

_____

_____

_____

_____

_____

What obstacles did you have to overcome?

_____

_____

_____

_____

_____

_____

Where can you see some walls coming down?

_____

_____

What is one thing of praise you received this week or learned that brought freedom or joy?

_____

_____

Thanksgiving

Jesus, you told your disciples, "Neither can you bear fruit unless you remain in me" (John 15:4). I remain in you by being attentive to the Holy Spirt and by accepting your help. I need it! I want to bear fruit, Jesus, but sometimes I really want to do everything on my own. I feel that temptation to strive to be a "perfect Christian" instead of opening my heart to trust in the Holy Spirit. May I trust more and more.

Scan this QR code for a free summary video from Phy!

ECCLESIOLOGY

A City on a Hill

KNOW WHAT
YOU BELIEVE.

LIVE IT
CONFIDENTLY.

COMMUNICATE
IT GRACIOUSLY.

ECCLESIOLOGY

Just a reminder: the exercises below are based on chapter seven: Ecclesiology in *EWAT*.

Opening Prayer

Jesus, I find this encouragement from Paul in his letter to the Ephesians, "And in him you too are being built together to become a dwelling in which God lives by his Spirit" (2:22). You are the cornerstone, and You are building us together into Your church. It is easy to get discouraged by the ups and downs of participating in church life. It can get very messy. As I study, renew my hope in Your church. You are the master builder, and we are in Your hands, becoming a holy dwelling place for Your Spirit.

Vocabulary Review

You certainly know the drill by now. I hope over the course of the study, you've come to appreciate how helpful it is to define our terms before we start talking theology. Defining terms can revolutionize the way you experience conversations in your church community and even with your spouse or close friends. Never think of the act of defining as too simple!

Ecclesiology: _____

Worship: _____

Know What You Believe

How to Navigate Tough Bible Passages

I have some unconventional advice when it comes to reading and understanding those really strange parts of the Bible like Leviticus. A portion of Leviticus is dedicated to instructing the Israelites what kinds of animals not to eat and what to do when they experience various ailments; you get the idea. It's a little outside of the box of your experience.

And that's okay.

Here's my advice: you don't have to apply every single verse of Scripture that you read. All of it is God's Word, and all of it is vital for building up the church. But you don't have to have an immediate, this-helps-me-understand-my-life-TODAY application for it. Truth be told, that's kind of a consumerist approach to the Bible.

You can use the same lens for your experiences at church. Maybe last Sunday wasn't exactly a banner Sunday. Maybe they didn't sing your favorite songs or the sermon didn't have much to do with your life or that family that you wanted to keep pursuing relationship with wasn't in the row in front of you. And yet your presence at church was still a response to God.

Maybe your Sunday was much worse than that. Maybe just showing up at church right now is hard for a whole host of legitimate reasons, but fellowshipping with other believers is still obedience. Especially if you're in a situation of spiritual abuse (there is more on this in chapter seven), you need to act, even going somewhere else for that fellowship. However, for every Christian, just like we show up for the tough Bible passages, we keep participating in worship with other believers, even when it is hard.

So don't let your growing habits of reading the Bible and studying the words be deterred by strangeness. Even if you can't apply what you've read in a specific way today, you are still holding and beholding God's holy Word.

As you go through odd passages, ask yourself four questions:

1. Where do I see God's heart here?

2. What are the deeper theological truths that still apply to us today, which lie behind the specific laws intended for Old Testament Israel?

3. Do I see any foretelling of the Messiah?

4. Who is God in this passage?

Instead of flipping past these passages, allow yourself to sit with them. Remember that these, too, are the words of God and they deserve our attention. As you go through them, make a place for them in your notebook, even if they don't have that aspect of immediate application. God's Word does not return to Him empty, and that includes Leviticus.

Head Knowledge

Church can be a really difficult topic. I bet you've had some amazing experiences at church. I bet you've also experienced a significant degree of "church hurt." As we go through this topic together, I want to acknowledge those highs and lows. I also want to inspire your heart. Church is so much more than those highs and lows. It goes beyond all of our personal experiences. Church is something that Jesus asks us to do together. That's why we do it—for Him. And when we're doing it for Him, we'll find that we have enough strength to do it together.

What four things about the church do we learn from the book of Acts?

_____

_____

What comes to your mind when you think of evangelism? According to Phy, what's the root of evangelism—where does that zeal come from?

_____

_____

Why did the apostles preach on unity so often?

What is Phy's definition of spiritual abuse? Have you ever experienced this?

Heart Change

Change in the church begins with change in our hearts. As we dig deeper into Scripture, we learn what the church is meant to be and to do. Hopefully, your experiences at church inspire you to study well. Your practice of study will also build up your church! Read through these questions before you get started. Start with the question that has a meaningful link into your day-to-day experiences. You'll know it when you see it.

Where does Christianity get its individualistic streak? Where do you see this pattern prevailing in the culture around you? What can Christians do to counteract individualism—what should that mode of being and thinking be replaced with?

The arc of church history trends away from isolation. Describe how the story of the church is a continuation of the story of Israel. What does God's call look like for Abraham, for Israel, and for the church? What links them together?

One Man: _____

One Nation: _____

The World: _____

_____

_____

_____

What does a "consumer" model of church look like? What does the "community" model of church look like? What are the ultimate results of each model?

_____

_____

_____

_____

_____

Theologian's Questions

What unanswered questions do you have about theology? What piqued your curiosity in this chapter? What caused confusion? Write these questions down so you can find out more by asking them to other believers or pursuing them in further research.

_____

_____

_____

_____

Common Ground

These questions are written for group discussion, but they can be used in individual study or as conversation starters. Church is all about common ground. Again, we don't have to agree on everything, but we do need to worship with other people. Remember the definition of worship from the chapter? Even discussion can be done in a way that makes it an act of worship as a body of believers.

What must a community do in order to be a Christian church? What kinds of things do not have any bearing on whether a community is a church?

_____

_____

How were the letters of the Bible meant to be read? How can church communities re-create that dynamic today? How do you think people would respond if you initiated that dynamic in your church, Bible study group, or family?

_____

_____

_____

What do the sacraments do for us? What sacraments does your church and/or tradition recognize?

_____

_____

_____

Which members of a church should be engaged in service? What does "service" look like? What makes service inauthentic?

_____

_____

_____

When it comes to life in the church, it's not *if* there will be tension, it's *when*. We have to decide what kinds of Christians we will be before the disagreement happens. What kinds of attitudes and actions can we build and exhibit to show who Christ is during tense times?

_____

_____

_____

Why is it so important to come together with other believers? What is the goal? Why not just listen to sermons at home or experience God's presence in nature?

_____

_____

_____

Live It Boldly

So . . . what are you going to DO about it?

Orthopraxy is the right practice of Christianity. It's the practice of living our beliefs boldly in our churches and in the world.

We spent the last several workbook chapters talking about theological triage—first-order issues like the nature of the Trinity, second-order issues like how to practice baptism, and third-order issues like best practices in parenting. It was important to break these out because, in order to commit to orthopraxy, we have to be grounded in what we believe and in what our priorities are. We must affirm the things the church has always affirmed while allowing the proper degrees of liberty in the lives of other believers.

Now, let's turn outward to the world. Let's start with this undeniable reality: God loves the world. That's why Jesus came to us in the first place! He came because of God's love, and He came to show God's love. The church exists because of God's love, but it also exists to love the world.

We don't always get this right. Read the section under theological triage: "The Threat Out There."

It can be really easy to see the world as a threat to our beliefs. But take heart, sisters: he has overcome the world. We do not need to be afraid of the people that Jesus is asking us to love. We can take refuge in our church communities, and we can serve and love each other in them (we should be doing that!), but we need to turn outward, too.

People resisted the love of Jesus. We should expect resistance, too. A friend might brush off our attempts to encourage her. A family member might remain totally disinterested in our invitations to church gatherings. Our city might not want us—"those church people"—helping out at a community outreach. These disappointments inevitably await us. We should respond with humility, patience, and trust in God's purpose and timing. No matter how many times we hear "no," we have to stay open to the possibilities in the future. We don't show Christ to the world when we view the world as the ultimate threat instead of the work of God's hands.

This week, write a prayer of opportunity for orthopraxy practice. It could be as simple as expressing this view in your own community— God wants us to love the world and not to view it as a threat.

Moving Forward

What worked well for you this week?

_____

_____

_____

_____

_____

What obstacles did you have to overcome?

_____

_____

_____

_____

_____

Where can you see some walls coming down?

_____

_____

What is one thing of praise you received this week or learned that brought freedom or joy?

_____

_____

Thanksgiving

As we live our lives as part of the church, help us to keep "our eyes on Jesus, the pioneer and perfecter of faith. For the joy set before him he endured the cross, scorning its shame, and sat down at the right hand of the throne of God" (Hebrews 12:2). Life in the church will offer us humiliation and hope. You knew both of those intimately. Help us all to remember that You are the pioneer and perfecter, and that You wanted us to do this together. Through Your Spirit and for the glory of Your Father, you give us strength to worship communally as Your church.

Scan this QR code for a free summary video from Phy!

ESCHATOLOGY

A New Heaven and a New Earth

KNOW WHAT
YOU BELIEVE.

LIVE IT
CONFIDENTLY.

COMMUNICATE
IT GRACIOUSLY.

ESCHATOLOGY

Just a reminder: the exercises below are based on chapter eight: Eschatology in *EWAT*.

Opening Prayer

Jesus, it's not over yet. You have more in store for me, and it is more wonderful than I can imagine. Paul wrote this to the Corinthians about the end of everything: "For now we see only a reflection as in a mirror; then we shall see face to face. Now I know in part; then I shall know fully, even as I am fully known" (1 Corinthians 13:12). I can look forward with hope, with joy, and with fearless trust in You, my Savior, who will make everything new and everything right. The end is a beginning, and You are in all of it.

Vocabulary Review

This is the last time we'll define terms in this workbook but consider how this practice can help you integrate theology into your walk with God and into your relationships with others. Terms create solid frameworks for conversations, especially when you're talking with someone who has a different perspective than you do. Find the terms in the chapter and write out the definitions.

Eschatology: _____

Exegesis: _____

Know What You Believe
How to Avoid Misapplying Scripture

Eschatology yields plentiful opportunities for the misapplication of Scripture—that is, applying a passage or several passages to our lives in wrongheaded ways, ways that God (and the authors of the books, letters, and poems) never intended. Revelation is a perfect example. The point of Revelation was to exalt God and demonstrate His victory over history, not to inspire fear in the hearts of believers. John expressed his vision to us in a way that reemphasizes the themes of his gospel and his letters: God's love overcomes everything.

It is surprisingly easy to misapply Scripture. We live in interesting times in an individualistic culture. With almost any piece of literature we read, we read it alone and we read it looking for a way to apply it to our lives right away. We must resist this urge when it comes to reading Scripture, or we'll make the mistakes of misapplication. We'll lose the larger story by looking for pieces that seem to have particular significance and interest for us. If we consistently use Scripture like this, one or more of these three things will probably happen:

1. *Limited view of God.* For example, Jeremiah 29:11 looks really good on an Instagram post: "For I know the plans I have for you . . ." However, if we don't know the larger context of those verses and we don't know anything about the prophet who wrote them, we will miss what he was saying about God—we won't get the full picture. If we miss on the part about the Babylonian exile, we'll miss the real depth of God's promise to the Israelites.

2. *Exalted view of self.* There is a lot of self-help literature out there, and some of it might actually be helpful. But the Bible is not a self-help book; it's the Word of God. And it's about Him, not about us, because that's actually what's best for us. If a Bible study or book keeps asking questions about you without asking any questions about him and his character, you should move on.

3. *Surface level understanding of Scripture.* No pain, no gain applies when it comes to reading God's Word. If you aren't puzzled or challenged by God's Word, you are probably sticking to the parts that feel easier to understand. But if you don't know the historical books of the Old Testament, you miss out on the richness of the gospel writer's use of history and culture of their people. Yes, Jesus is your Savior, but what did "messiah" mean to the people who walked with Jesus? It's worth finding out, which means it's worth weathering some "drier" passages Scripture. God will still meet you there, especially in the middle of the passages that challenge you.

So, how do you avoid misapplying Scripture? A great place to start is to do the reverse of these three dangers of misapplication. On the whole, it means reading the Bible as though it is about Him. Pursue the larger context of the passages you're reading, asking God for more information from His Word. Each time you start your study, start by asking God to show you more of who He is. And never settle for a surface level understanding. If you find yourself glazing over some of the verses that you don't understand, rejoice. That means there is more of Him to know, and all of eternity to find out.

Head Knowledge

Apocalyptic scenarios are everywhere these days and, almost without exception, these "end-of-the-world" media extravaganzas involve mass chaos, destruction, and fear. People seem to derive a lot of significance from the idea that the end of the world could happen soon, and Christians are no exception. Even we can get caught up in the hype. That said, it's quite possible that your encounter with eschatology and what the Bible actually says about the end times have been parallel instead of convergent—that is, what you've heard about the end isn't actually what He said. Let's find out together.

What comes to mind when you hear the word "revelation"? What emotions and experiences specifically?

_____

_____

_____

Have you ever misunderstood a symbol or watched someone misunderstand a symbol? What happened next? What happens when we aren't familiar with the symbols that are being used?

_____

_____

What are the four eschatological views, and what is each view identified by?

What do all four eschatological perspectives agree on?

Heart Change

Our hearts should long for heaven; our hearts long to be united with God. That's what they were created for. Yet, when many of us hear the words "Judgment Day," we internally quake or cringe. Fear and anxiety surround the discussion about the end times, even though we know that God has promised a new heaven and a new earth. This is a good promise! As you dig deep into eschatology, ask God to replace any fear or anxiety with hope and trust. Remember, you're wrestling, not answering questions on a test. Start with the question that has the most to do with your day-to-day experiences. You'll know it when you see it.

The book of Daniel contains prophecies that parallel the account in Revelation; so does John 14. Look up either of these passages. Do either of them bring to light anything that you hadn't thought of before when reading Revelation? What are the similarities?

Think about how the four eschatological views would influence the way a person thought about a specific key word. You can choose one of the following below or choose your own word.

CHURCH   JUDGMENT   HOPE

Historical/Covenant Premillennialism

_____

_____

Amillennialism

_____

_____

Postmillennialism

_____

_____

Dispensational Premillennialism

_____

_____

The way a believer views the end times will affect the way that they act in the present. What kinds of views will inspire evangelism, service, and charity?

_____

_____

Theologian's Questions

What unanswered questions do you have about theology? What piqued your curiosity in this chapter? What caused confusion? Write these questions down so you can find out more by asking them to other believers or pursuing them in further research.

Common Ground

These questions are written for group discussion, but they can be used in individual study or as conversation starters. Eschatology can create incredible opportunities for conversation. You can't find a topic much more interesting than the end of the world! As you discuss these together, make hope the cornerstone of the conversation. God has promised that He will make everything right—what could be better than that?

What vision comes to mind when you think of heaven, and what (or who) do you think influenced that vision? Does your vision depict activity or inactivity?

Fear is a major player in the *Left Behind* series and other types of a cultural milieu that discuss the end of the world. What other topics inspire a concentration on fear? Why is fear so prevalent when it comes to the end of the world?

What was God's purpose in telling people about the end of the world? Why did He include these prophecies in the Bible? What was He trying to do?

How did dispensational premillennialism spread throughout the church? What does hopeful premillennialism look like? What does fearful premillennialism look like?

What would you say to someone who argued that a God who loved would not judge? Think about the relationship between love and justice.

Allow yourselves to imagine what heaven will be like. Ask God to give you hope. Think of the adventure that life with Christ can be here and now. What might that adventure be like when everything has been rectified and restored?

Live It Boldly

So . . . what are you going to DO about it?

Orthopraxy is the right practice of Christianity. It's the practice of living our beliefs boldly in our churches and in the world.

We've come to the end of the book and the end of the study by discussing the end of all things. Now, turn to the very end of the conclusion in the book and read the section called "Students of the Heart of God."

The result of theology is hope in all things—yes, all things! Even in eschatology, the theme coursing through the study of God's heart is hope. In everything we've studied, there is tremendous hope from the Bible to the Holy Spirit, from the creation of the world to the institution of the church: HOPE. Maybe studying these things didn't result in the same pulse-quickening experience that hearing your favorite worship song or rereading familiar passages does, but I pray that your study will draw you deeper into your understanding of how great He is. I pray that the fruit of your study is *hope* in everything—in your job, with your family, with your friends, and with the world.

You are called to be a lover of God and to draw close to Him. And I hope that you are now more accustomed to a title that I believe becomes you very well: Theologian.

Moving Forward

What worked well for you this week?

_____

_____

_____

_____

_____

What obstacles did you have to overcome?

_____

_____

_____

_____

_____

Where can you see some walls coming down?

_____

_____

What is one thing of praise you received this week or learned that brought freedom or joy?

_____

_____

Thanksgiving

Peter wrote in his second letter, "The Lord is not slow in keeping his promise, as some understand slowness. Instead he is patient with you, not wanting anyone to perish, but everyone to come to repentance" (2 Peter 3:9). You are patient and loving and faithful to Your people. You promised that all things would end, that You would return, and that everything would be new. Because of what You've promised in Your Word, I can wait with great hope. I can look toward the end of everything and see the magnificence of Your love.

Come, Lord Jesus!

Scan this QR code for a free summary video from Phy!

APPENDIX

Vocabulary List
(Definitions are found in the *EWAT* book.)

Lesson One

theology: the study of the nature of God and his truth (page ix)

humanism: a worldview focused on the rational and material rather than the divine or supernatural (page xiii)

bibliology: the theology about the Bible (page 2)

canon: a collection of books able to tell us who God is and how we should live in relationship to Him (page 6)

genre: a type of literary composition (page 8)

Lesson Two

orthodoxy: right or sound teachings about Christianity (page 170)

orthopraxy: right practice of Christianity (page 170)

Lesson Three

cosmology: the study of the origin and purpose of the universe (page 44)

theism: a belief in God/a god or a creator who is personally involved in his creation (page 45)

anthropology: the study of humanity's origin, nature, and destiny (page 48)

hamartiology: the study of sin's definition, effects, and redemption (page 48)

Lesson Four

Christology: the study of Christ's character, humanity, deity, and future return (page 64)

incarnation: when the eternal God put on a human nature, body, and person called Jesus, the Greek name for Hebrew Joshua (page 70)

Lesson Five

soteriology: the study of Christian salvation from sin (page 89)

sanctification: the living out of our holy identity, progressively becoming more like Jesus (page 104)

glorification: the final removal of sin from God's people (page 107)

Lesson Six

pneumatology: the study of the Holy Spirit (page 111)

Lesson Seven

ecclesiology: the theology of the church, its mission, and its structure (page 132)

worship: attributing honor, attention, reverence, and focus to God (page 138)

Lesson Eight

eschatology: theology of the final things (page 150)

exegesis: drawing out the intended and accurate meaning of a text (page 154)

Using This Workbook in a Group Study: A Brief Guide

Dear Leader,

Hello again!

It's Phy.

Thank you so much for choosing to engage with me in *EWAT*. I'm writing this letter specifically to those of you who want to use *EWAT* and the companion workbook as a group study.

Sounds like you're thinking about starting a group. That's amazing. Again, thank you for considering my book. But, so much more than that, thank you for extending your heart in hospitality to other women. Whatever you choose to do, I'm praying that all of you would know and love Jesus more, and that you would experience His love in a new way through your journey as a leader.

If you decide to use the book and workbook for *Every Woman a Theologian* for a group study, here are some suggestions I'd make. Every woman in your group will complete personal, individual study on the material before you come together to discuss it as a group. There are supplementary videos which correspond to each chapter where I give the highlights and overarching reference points of each doctrine. These would be a great thing to watch at the end of your group meetings to recap and prepare for your next week.

Who do you invite? Well, women you esteem. You don't all have to be at the same place spiritually, or even go to the same church, but there does need to be mutual respect. You could even invite friends from different "circles." The point is, you need to be a group of women that wants to take your practice of theology from head knowledge to heart change. So who should join you? Take that to prayer. Ask the Holy Spirit to work in your mind as you think about who to invite. Then, invite. And invite with an open heart and hand.

So, does your group need to have a pre-lesson? Here are a few questions to help you decide. Is your group an established group or a new one? Do you have some new women joining you? Are these ladies familiar with Bible study, or are you not quite sure where people are at? Depending on these factors, you might benefit from a pre-lesson. I'm talking about a very casual gathering where your group discusses the gameplan for the study. Maybe you need that or maybe you need to dive right into the content. Invite the Holy Spirit into this decision, and then act with confidence!

Lesson One content will start right in with the introduction and the first chapter of *Every Woman a Theologian*. Each chapter is about twenty pages long and includes in-depth content. In order to complete the workbook material, you have to read the corresponding chapter. You could read the chapter with your workbook open or peruse the workbook questions before diving into the chapter. A weekly meeting could be a great rhythm for this study.

I'd recommend that members of your group read and complete each section of whichever lesson you are on individually before meeting together, with the exception of the common ground questions. Those questions are aimed at groups and will serve to guide your discussion. Investing your time in the material before you get together is going to improve the quality of your conversation, and it's going to prepare your heart to listen and learn from other women.

Here's a sample study schedule:

Weekly, members complete the reading individually, guided by the workbook.

At Group:

Opening Prayer: Always begin in prayer, thanking God for your group and the time to study.

First Impressions: Ask for first impressions—things that surprised people or really struck their hearts.

Common Ground Questions: The workbook provides six common ground questions—use these to guide your discussion or inspire new questions.

Theologian's Questions: Bring up individual questions that came up during the reading.

Video: If you'd like, use the video that corresponds to the chapter to recap the lesson.

Encouragement: Ask how the process of study went and encourage each other. Make sure everyone knows which chapter is being read for the next meeting. Share prayer requests.

Closing Prayer: Close in prayer, thanking God and praising Him.

The flow of personal study and group discussion will be different for each group. Ask for the right balance of openhandedness and persistence. Allow your group to be guided by the Holy Spirit. By choosing this study, you and I are partnering together on a mission: to help women know what they believe and live it boldly.

Committing to group study is committing to wrestling with truth. Entering into community like this will challenge your assumptions and grow your faith. For the sake of everyone involved, there will be moments of discomfort and moments of real joy. You will hear about experiences that are different than your own and embark on a new journey of understanding. Pray for the grace to grow together well.

You are an incredible leader. Thank you for giving your heart and your time!

Phy

Companion book
to enrich your
study experience

Available wherever books are sold.

From the Publisher

GREAT STUDIES

ARE EVEN BETTER WHEN THEY'RE SHARED!

Help others find this study:

- Post a review at your favorite online bookseller.

- Post a picture on a social media account and share why you enjoyed it.

- Send a note to a friend who would also love it—or, better yet, go through it with them!

Thanks for helping others grow their faith!

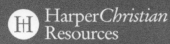